An Extraordinary
God
In an Ordinary Life

BY
BILLY GENE ROBERTS

Copyright © 2023 by Billy Gene Roberts

All rights reserved.

All rights reserved. No part of this publication may be reproduced, distributed, or transmitted in any form or by any means, including photocopying, recording, or other electronic or mechanical methods, without the prior written permission of the author of the book, except in the form of brief quotations embodied in critical reviews and specific other noncommercial purposes permitted by copyright law.

"Most incredible, however, are the times we know He is with us in the midst of our daily, routine lives. In the middle of cleaning the house or driving somewhere in the pickup, He stops us......in our tracks and makes His presence known. Often, it's in the middle of the most mundane tasks that He lets us know he is there with us. We realize, then that there can be no "ordinary" moments for people who live their lives with Jesus."

Max Lacado

Note to Readers:

This book was written initially for my family. My reasons are noted in at the beginning of the book. There are names that are easily familiar to my family, but as an outside reader, I would like to explain the names.

My mother was named Martha. When I was in high school, I took Spanish, and we used to call my dad Senor and my mother Senorita. Over the years her name was shortened to "Rita", and everyone called her that for years. I am not sure my grandkids know to this day her real name was Martha. Other names: Robbie, my oldest daughter; Staci, my youngest daughter; Johnny, my middle brother, and Tommy, my youngest brother; "Pops" (that's me), and my wonderful wife, Shari.

Table of Contents

CHAPTER ONE
AN EXTRAORDINARY GOD IN AN ORDINARY LIFE

I have decided I would try to capture many of the interactions between me and God in my life. I just wanted my children and grandchildren to know how Extraordinary God is in our lives if we only take time to look at his actions. Many times, it is only in retrospect that we see his presence. Things that seem random are really well orchestrated by God, and at my age, I see his presence more clearly in what I thought were ordinary, even random events. I no longer believe anything is a coincidence. You don't have to be my age for this to happen and that is why I wanted to take time to share this with you now so you might appreciate Him now in your "ordinary" life. It may sound crazy getting a little book from me, but it's important for me to tell you how extraordinary God has made my ordinary life. And he is doing the same in yours. Most of what is written here you have never heard before, but in seeing God's hand in so much of my life, I just felt I wanted to tell somebody, so I chose my family. I hope you can find the time to read it and apply the principle that God is in every situation, no matter how ordinary you think it is. There are no coincidences.

CHAPTER TWO
THE BEGINNING

I grew up in a home with two loving parents and two brothers. Our lives were very middle class normal. Life was very different for children then as we had to really use our imaginations to entertain ourselves. We would make up all kinds of games and adventures with just what we had in our surroundings. What I remember so much was our vacations to Florida. We used to get up at 4 am, pack in the non air-conditioned car and drive to Panama City Beach. We would stay for two weeks in a cottage across the street from the beach. Most days, my brother and I were up at 6 am and ready to spend the entire day at the beach. The refrigerator was an icebox, so we had to buy a block of ice that went in the refrigerator to keep things cold. It was not electric. A big night out would be going to putt putt golf or to the roller coaster park. Most days were just spent at the beach, and we loved it. It was there that I fell in love with the ocean. All my life,

I have wanted to live by the ocean and in April 2004, God made that dream come true. I now live in Santa Rosa Beach, Fl. To this day, I try to go to the beach at least every afternoon just for a quick swim and walk down the beach just to enjoy the beauty. The reason I love the ocean so much is because I believe when I stand on the beach and look at the ocean, I am looking at the very same view God had when he created the earth. I don't believe that view has changed since the beginning of time and I am seeing it just as God did when he said…"It is Good." God planted something in me that would be a lifelong love affair with his creation…the ocean.

These vacation memories are so sweet that even today, I drive to the location of the old cottage, which is gone, and walk over the same beach path that I, Johnny, Tommy, Rita, and Daddy (my family) walked. It's like going back in time to a cherished memory. There is a donut shop that was by our cottage, and it is still there even 65 years later.

One memory also is burned into my mind. Birmingham was very segregated, and blacks and whites did not associate. Whites, thought they were better than blacks. I was raised in this culture, and I guess I just accepted that being white, I was better than blacks. Oddly enough, we had a black woman who came and lived with us when my brothers were born to help Rita take care of the baby and Rita. Her name was Ada. I remember looking at her hands and seeing the palms were whiter than the rest of her skin. I asked her why she didn't wash the rest of her body, like the palm of her hands so she would be a white person instead of black….Rita tells me that she got the biggest laugh out of that, as did Ada. But the memory I am speaking of that is so burned in my mind was when I went to the first McDonald's in Birmingham which was by my house. I was eight years old. It was nothing nice like they are today, kind of trashy, actually.

A very well-dressed black couple came in with two daughters. They had been to church and were well dressed. They tried to order but were refused service.

The manager finally said if they would go to the back door, which had a bunch of trash cans near it, they could be served there. The husband and wife looked so dejected, so hurt, so embarrassed. Right then, God put in my heart that this was wrong. These people did not deserve to be treated differently. They were nice. What he put in my heart was permanent, and I will never forget the feeling. God was speaking to me clearly, although I may not have recognized it was HIM. People of all colors are made by Him and they are precious and should be treated so.

CHAPTER THREE
THINGS CHANGE

My Dad had been sick for several years, but when I was about eight he became totally disabled with chronic relapsing pancreatitis and heart problems. Rita did not work because women stayed home and raised children in those days. Money became a big problem over the next 13+ years. Rita did come up with the idea to make clowns out of old bowling pins which she sold. She also typed addresses for a penny and a label to keep us from starving. My Dad was sick for about 13+ years, and she had to constantly care for him some days. She also had to care for three growing boys, which was a handful. So many nights after everyone would go to bed, she would start working on painting her little bowling pin clowns, which she painted in different college colors and sold for two dollars apiece. It probably took her about 2 hours to make one bowling pin clown. She sold hundreds of them. She would work until the wee hours of the morning, knowing she would have to get up early, get us off to school, and begin her care of my Dad. When not making clowns, she would type things called stencils, which were used to make address labels. She got one penny for each stencil. I can still see her sitting at the dining room table late at night, trying to make money to feed us and pay household expenses. My mother was a saint, and I will never be able to express my gratitude for her selfless sacrifice for the family. I didn't know it at the time, but God was showing me the sacrifice someone will make for you when they love you. I could never thank her enough in a million years for what she did.

I remember being close to losing our house, and just in time, someone would give us money to make the house payment. I remember one time when we were about to lose the house, a neighbor knocked on the door and said, "Something just told me I needed to give you this money. I don't know why, but I feel I am supposed to give it to you." It was what we needed for the house payment. I now see these gifts as God working to save our house.

I remember one Thanksgiving when my brothers and I were playing football and Rita was making Thanksgiving lunch in the kitchen. The doorbell rang, and there were people from our church with all kinds of food for Thanksgiving. Rita busted out crying, but I didn't understand what would make her cry. What I later found out was the time she was in the kitchen, she was praying God would send us some food because we did not have anything for Thanksgiving. She wasn't cooking anything, just praying. God provided for my family that day, and I later realized through that incident that God does perform miracles.

I was a baseball player, and I loved the game. I was starting catcher on all my little league teams and made the All-Stars every year. One year, we were in the playoff game to go to the Little League World Championship. Unfortunately, we lost against a fantastic pitcher. I also played what was called Pony League when I was 13, 14, and 15, along with high school baseball. I was the starting catcher on all my teams.

Because of our money problems, Rita took in work at home typing and making these little clowns from bowling pins. I had to go to work in the summer full time to help out when I was 14. I had to get a special child labor permit because most kids my age did not work full-time. I worked in a foundry, which was hot dirty work. Because of that, I could not make baseball practice much, and my game deteriorated. I tried to hide the fact I had to work because the other kids did not have to, and I was embarrassed.

I always had some excuse for missing practice. I remember one time, after a bad night at the plate, the coach said, "That's what you get for not coming to practice." I didn't want to tell him I had to work because I was embarrassed about working, but it really hurt my feelings. At 15, I realized that I could not continue baseball because I needed to work. The full-time work was just in the summer, so I could play high school baseball, and I was the starting catcher. We won the city championship one year. Still, I had to work on the weekends to help the family. One time, the coach called a practice on a Saturday, which we never did. I never got the message about the special practice, or I would have tried to get off work (I was a grocery sacker) to practice. That Monday, my coach kicked me off the team for missing that one practice. I tried to explain that I did not know about the practice and I may have had to work anyway, but I would have made every effort to be there. He was a short little cocky guy with a Napoleon complex. He had no sympathy and kicked me off. High school was the only baseball I could play because of the summer work. I hate that son of bitch coach to this day.

Still, what I did not realize through this difficulty of trying to play baseball and work, God was teaching me a strong work ethic. I realized I needed an education because I didn't want to do hard labor all my life, and I wanted to succeed. Working in that dirty foundry taught me a lot of things. A strong work ethic was implanted in me by God. After college, I had a couple of jobs but joined a company in the clinical laboratory business that had only 175 employees in 4 states. When I left in December 2003, I had been a part of growing that company to 25,000 employees that was nationwide. We were a Fortune 500 company. I had moved through the ranks from Branch manager of one office to Regional Vice President of Operations for 4 years and Regional Vice President of sales for 12 years. At the end of my career, I was in charge of a one-billion-dollar territory. Every year, we had an awards trip for the top performers in the company. These were very luxurious trips to beautiful resorts. I was the only Sales Officer to be invited to every Sales Reward trip. At the 50th anniversary of the company's founding, Shari and I were picked as one of the top 50 people who had built the company, and we received an award at the 50th-anniversary celebration. I also was blessed financially so Shari and I could retire when I was 55. This allowed me to fulfill my dream of living at the beach and, most importantly, have time to spend with my grandchildren. Absolutely Priceless. I attribute the early working years that God put me through at the sacrifice of baseball for giving me a strong work ethic that rewarded me more than I could have ever dreamed of. God was using lessons from that old dirty foundry to teach me about life in business and how to treat people who would make me a success. It all seemed so ordinary and even unfair (baseball) at the time, but God was teaching me lessons about life in business and how to treat people, which is basically the Golden Rule.

Because of God's financial blessings, we retired early, and it was so great because we got to spend time with our grandchildren. We had so much fun at the beach with them. We all loved to play "Deadliest Catch" in the ocean and do all kinds of things at the beach and beach club. We loved going to Shipwreck Island too. Because I always loved the ocean so much, I guess I secretly wanted to let them have a lot of fun in the water playing, doing snorkeling trips and dolphin trips so maybe they would love the ocean like I do. Those years with young grandchildren were some of the happiest times of my life. I just can't thank God enough for giving me the time and money to spend their early years with us.

The grandchildren have almost grown up now, and we rarely see them at the beach anymore. We miss that, but we understand that they have their own lives now. I wouldn't have it any other way because some people have children who have disabilities, and the child can never really grow up. I am so glad my grandchildren are healthy and normal. Spending less time with their grandparents is just a normal part of them growing up because they are finding their own lives and they are busy. Still, sometimes, in my dreams, I wish I had my little "playmates" again.

Chapter Four
God's Promise is True

I always wanted to go to Auburn University. In my senior year, I applied and was accepted. In the spring, before school started in September, Rita sat me down and said we have no money to send you to college. I knew that in my heart, but my mom and Dad did a great job of protecting us from how bad things were financially, so I thought the college money would be there somehow. It was not. I was desperate, and as a last resort, I turned to God. I remember reading in Sunday school that if you give 10% of your money to the church, God will bless you financially. So, I challenged God. It was not a step of faith; it was a challenge to see if what he said was true. In June (school started mid-September), I decided I would give 10% of my paycheck to the church and see if God could give me what I needed to go to Auburn. I made $48 a week (still in the foundry). Each week, I gave $4.80 to West End Methodist Church, my 10% tithe.

Most of the rest went to help the family. I was saying. "Ok, God, let's see what you can do with that promise of yours." I needed $1200 per semester for tuition and board and I had nothing. In July, the Federal Government started the Federal Student Loan Progarm for the first time ever and I applied. I was awarded $600 per semester in government loans. One half of what I would need. In very late August, I still did not have the other half. One day, our Life Insurance man stopped by and Rita mentioned my situation and it looked like I was not going to be able to go to Auburn. He said, "I know George Wallace, and Governor of Alabama. I will call him and see what we can do." He returned and said limited funds were available for students with good grades who were in financial hardship. He said the fund was running out fast, so I had to hurry to apply. I applied immediately, and with 1.5 weeks of school starting, I got a $600 per semester scholarship.....JUST THE EXACT amount I needed. So God came through in short order. He lived up to his promise with little time to work with. I got to go to Auburn. His promise was true.

While I am speaking of money and tithing, I will share another story that made me a 100% believer in tithing.

After watching God miraculously provide money for me to go to Auburn through tithing, I did not tithe for over 20 years. I am sure that hurt his feelings since he came through for me, but I forgot about giving back to him (at least tithing) as soon as I got out of college. At age 42, we were challenged, as usual, to tithe during our annual campaign fund at Riverchase Presbyterian church. I had ignored these in past years, thinking I still gave a lot. This time was different. God was really speaking to me to tithe. Shari and I were doing very well financially at the time but still looking at two teenage daughters going to college, for which we had little preparation. I figured I was giving so much that tithing would be an easy addition. Then I looked at the numbers and found I was giving 2%! That was it. Holy smokes, how could we increase 8%? That was quadrupling our giving! That was a very large amount to increase to 10%.

At first, I rationalized that I needed to save for the girls' college since it was only 2 to 3 years away, and we had little saved for that. God kept speaking to me to trust him. Trusting God is very hard when it comes to putting your money where your mouth is. But we did it. We signed the pledge cards in November and started our tithing in January. As luck would have it, the company put a nationwide freeze on raises indefinitely in January, so it looked like no raises to help offset the church donation. Raises were not going to come close to making up the money, but they would have helped. Then, in late February, God made his move. First, with 25,000 people not getting raises, Shari was called in and given a special project from the President of the company. In addition, despite the wage freeze, this project was so important that she got a big raise. THE ONLY PERSON OUT OF 25,000 PEOPLE TO BE ALLOWED A RAISE. In addition, a study had been done, and the company found it was paying female officers much less than male officers. They corrected that by also giving Shari a HUGE raise. Ok, you won't believe this, but it is true. When we got the first check reflecting these raises, the amount of the raise was EXACTLY the amount that we had added to our giving to tithe 10%. Basically, God gave us all our money back. It was unbelievable. I GUESS YOU COULD SAY God is always unbelievable.

CHAPTER FIVE
DIVORCE

Gail and I were married for 12 years and had two precious daughters. Much of that time was a happy time, but we married way too young. I was 21 by 3 weeks, and she was 19. We were immature in relationships, and over the years, we grew apart. I do not blame her at all. We just changed during those married years and we let our love die. We had many happy times together, which is what I choose to remember. She is a wonderful mother, and I will always love her for how she has cared for our children. Robbie and Staci are two of the greatest things we ever did and the world is better off because of these two beautiful girls. We have something to be very proud of.

I was single for 6 years and Gail was single for about the same time, but God put perfect mates into our lives. We were both blessed with new spouses that were absolutely perfect for each of us. Gail and I were both more mature and understood more about relationships, so we did a better job of being a Husband and a Wife. I am so happy that we are friends and would do anything to help each other, and I am so glad Shari and Jim are good friends too. God has ways to mend our hearts and teach us from our mistakes. One thing I will credit both of us on during the divorce was we focused on what was best for the children. Each of us sacrificed things just to make the children be OK. I remember one of the teachers at school telling one of us (not sure which) that they could always tell when a child's family was going through a divorce, but with Robbie and Staci, they did not know it because we did everything possible to make their lives normal. "All things work for good for those that love the Lord."

One great thing that came out of this difficult period was I found a personal relationship with Jesus. I had always heard the term, but I didn't realize until I went through many agonizing nights over the divorce just how honest I became with Jesus. I had always believed, but now I depended on him more. Through this time, I realized that a personal relationship with God means you involve him in EVERY aspect of your life, even the little things. It also means I became "God Conscious." Whenever I saw beauty in nature, I took time to thank Him. Whenever I saw a disabled person, I would pray that minute for them. Sometimes, I would just thank God I could see, hear, talk, think, etc. Stuff people take for granted became things I always involved God in. We were "personal" friends, and I wanted to talk with Him about every little thing. That was a change from the way I dealt with him before.

CHAPTER SIX
WHY I BELIEVE IN GOD

Still, divorce was the most traumatic event of my life. To this day, I don't want to look at the file I have on the divorce. It brings up heartache. During the early days after divorce, I was terrified I would lose the children. All I heard were stories of women and men who divorced and used their children as weapons against each other. I was afraid she would remarry and move away, or I would be replaced as their Dad. I was petrified of losing my children.

In June 1981, I took the girls to Navarre Beach, FL. It was the first time I had been on such a trip with just me and them. They were playing all the way down, and in those days, you could get up in the back window, which they liked to do. We played all kinds of games and they were laughing all the way. But with every laugh, I kept thinking, what if all this goes away...what if I lose them? I was so afraid. When we got to the Holiday Inn Holidome in Navarre Beach, Florida, we went for a walk on the beach. It was cloudy and not many people were out. The girls were running ahead of me, laughing and playing in the water's edge. Again, this was so bittersweet because I wanted them to laugh, but I was terrified the laughter would be taken from me. I turned to God and asked him to please keep them close, but I couldn't wait years to see how this panned out. I needed to know now! I asked God to give me a sign that they would always be close. I know this sounds stupid, but to make sure I knew the sign, I told God what the sign should be (he must have laughed)....me telling him what to do. I asked him to let me find three whole white sand dollars as we walked along, and I would know that would be the sign that everything would be OK. I promised God that if he did this, I would raise them in the church and teach them about Him. Here is what I did not realize when I asked for this. The only sand dollars I had seen were in the souvenir store, and they were white. I thought that was how they came in nature. Wrong. Sand dollars are gray in nature; they only become white by laying in the shallow surf and being bleached by the sun. They are almost always crushed by the waves, so a whole one is very rare. What I was asking for was 3 of these extremely rare creatures, and I didn't know what a miracle it would be to find one whole white sand dollar, much less three. Within about 20 or 30 seconds of praying this prayer, I looked down, and laying in the surf were 3 WHOLE, WHITE, SAND DOLLARS!! They were in a perfect row like little soldiers. I was shocked!!! As I recall, it seemed that my breath had been taken away. I grasped for air for a moment. It just couldn't be…but they were there. With shaky hands, I reached down to pick them up, still wondering if I was looking at a mirage. They were there. All three. I will never forget the feeling of a miracle put at my feet. A God so gracious that he helped a terrified child and erased my pain. What was even greater was that the girls and I remained very close. I had them every weekend and I did take them to church every Sunday. I also had them some Wednesday nights. We were very close, just as God had promised. This is amazing that an Extraordinary God would do such a thing for such an ordinary person. If I had never read a bible, if I had never been to church, never recognized all

God has done for me, I would and will always believe in
God because of this one day…this one extraordinary day.

CHAPTER SEVEN
GOD AND WORK

I started noting way earlier, the success I had in my career, but believe me, every day was filled prayers when I needed help surviving work. I worked in a company that was open 24-7, 365 days a year. We never closed so there were always problems at all hours of the day, night and weekends. We were also publicly traded on the stock exchange so no matter how good we did financially, it was never enough. The pressure was relentless.

In the mid-nineties we merged with our most fierce competitor. Neither company liked each other. The other company had a reputation for ruthlessness and firing people at will. The merger was complete turmoil and almost brought our company down. Despite getting one name we operated like two different companies, with their philosophy in some parts of the country and ours in others. There were always clashes and we never seemed to be able to become one unified organization.

In 2002, my division, which was run like our old company, was merged into another division, run by a guy from the other company. The guy from the other company was put in charge of everything. He had a reputation for being ruthless and firing people routinely. When we merged these two divisions, that meant there were two Regional Sales officers and we only needed one. I was one of the sales Officers and a girl who had worked for this other guy for years was the other. They were very close and I was an outsider from the other company. Their offices had been side by side for years. He called us both into his office one day and said in 6 months, one of you will be gone. What no one knew was I planned to retire in 15 months, but I needed to stay those 15 months to get my retirement medical benefits. Now, I am being told I could be let go within six months and lose my retirement. I was shocked that this could possibly happen.

To stack the deck in favor of the lady sales officer, the Senior V.P. took St. Louis away from her and gave it to me. St. Louis had been a company business "shithole" for many years. No one could penetrate the market, and I knew he wanted me to have it so he could set me up to fail and keep her. Believe me, I prayed so much for God's help because everyone prior to me for 20 years had failed. I hired a new salesperson and I spent an enormous amount of time selling there myself. Our biggest competitor had a regional lab there and all we had was a branch office. The competitor had all the big accounts in St. Louis and they just assumed they would keep them. Whenever there was a big bid, the competitor would send a salesman or a customer service person to the bid because they thought they would automatically get the business. I, a Vice President, would show up for our company and it made an impression that we really cared. I prayed so much that God would open doors and he did. We ended up getting the largest accounts in the city and our business boomed!...thanks be to God. We have many more big and important accounts. Instead of ending up being the 'Goat" like the boss wanted, I was a hero!...again, thanks be to God. What was meant for bad turned out to be very good for me.

I learned through another senior V.P. that my V.P. (who was trying to get rid of me) told all the executive management at a meeting that his girl Vice president had laid all the groundwork, and I had walked in and got the business because of what she had done. This pissed me off. My boss was a bully and liked to fire people because he thought it made him look tough. I didn't give a damn. I picked up the phone and called him and confronted him with what he said. I was almost yelling; I was so mad. Here I am basically chewing out my boss, who was a badass! He cowered down and denied that he had said anything like that. He was humble pie, but I knew the bastard was lying. Still, it is only by the grace of God that I did not get fired (right before my retirement) because of my temper. I rarely lose my temper, but when I do, I will cut my own throat to bleed on you!!

CHAPTER EIGHT
GOD AND MY MOTHER

My Mom and Dad took me to church and I know that is where I found God, although the relationship was immature, as I would learn later when I gained a personal relationship with Him. I am so thankful for my mom and Dad taking me to church. It was the beginning of life eternal.

My mother had some experiences that reinforced to me that God exists and does miraculous things. Hearing God's work in others reinforces my faith.

As noted, my Dad was sick for many years. One night, he was having a hard time and my mother just told God for the first time that she would let him go if that was His wish. He died the next day after many years of sickness.

One night shortly after my Dad died, she said a voice woke her up in the middle of the night. The voice was clear and spoke just like a person speaking to her. The voice said, "But first seek his kingdom and his righteousness and all these things will be given to you as well." She said it was no dream; she was wide awake. That verse stuck with me and at my retirement party, when people were talking about how "great" I was, I acknowledged that my successes were all a credit to God and I quoted that verse.

One day, my mother was on a latter painting and she fell backward from the top of the latter. "Someone" unseen caught her and gently laid her on the floor. It was an angel.

The most dramatic experience with God that my mother had was when she played a role in saving a man's life. She was driving down the road and she said it felt like her car was gently picked up and laid in a ditch. She was shocked. Stunned at how she got there with no crash or damage. A man came up to the car to check on her as he saw what happened. He said he had a winch on his truck and he could pull her out of the ditch. He did so and she thanked him so much and said she just didn't understand how it happened. The man said, "Ma'am I am the one that should thank you. You see, on the seat of my truck is a shotgun and I was on my way to kill myself when I saw you go off the road. I helped you and now I know I still have value and can do good things. I now want to live, not die." No doubt an angel orchestrated that incident using Mother to save that man's life.

CHAPTER NINE
GOD'S HEALING

In 2008, Shari was diagnosed with breast cancer. We found out 4 days before Christmas. It was scary, but she had a small surgery and radiation treatment. We had a trip planned to Disney World with Robbie's family, which fell right in the middle of her radiation treatment. She got permission to miss a few days to go on the trip. The trip was great, but that black cloud was hanging over our heads. Shari acted like it did not even bother her, so the trip would be normal. I was proud of her. They also gave her a chemotherapy pill that she really did not need. Shari was always tiny, but this medicine made her gain about 25 pounds. She told the doctor she was stopping the medicine because of this and the effect on her liver, but it changed her metabolism, so she has never been able to lose the weight. They should have never given her that medicine. Still, when something like this happens, you think, *what if I lose her?* I prayed so much to God during this time and he did heal her. She has had a few scares since then, but they were all scar tissue from the radiation, no tumors. She is completely healed and cured. I am so thankful to God for saving her.

In 2013, I was diagnosed with prostate cancer. This is diagnosed by a test called PSA, which is usually high when you have prostate cancer. Mine was totally normal, but because it took a jump in the normal range, my great doctor checked me for it, and sure enough, I had it. I am so thankful to God for giving me this great doctor. The treatment for early prostate cancer is surgical removal. When I found out, I said let's get the little bastard out of there right now. The doctor told me I had to wait 6 weeks for the prostate to heal from the biopsy. Six weeks! I want it gone now, but that was not in the cards. I had many sleepless nights worrying about this over that period of time and I am sure I worried God until he was sick of hearing from me. I was fearful and wanted it over even though my prognosis was very good.

Every morning, I read a bible verse that pops up on my iPad from my Bible app. The app randomly chooses what verse comes up. I have no control over it. One morning, a few weeks before the surgery, I was sitting on my porch, ready to open the app. I told God I was in desperate need of hearing from Him that everything was going to be ok. I wasn't sleeping well, and it was always on my mind and I had weeks to go before the surgery. Before opening the app, I asked God to send me his message to comfort me and that everything was going to be ok. There are 31,102 verses in the Bible, so what are the odds that the one that comes up will be an answer to my prayer? When I opened the app, the verse was from Isaiah 41:10

"Do not be afraid, I am with you!

I am your God, let nothing terrify you

I will make you strong and help you

I will protect you and save you."

I could hardly believe my eyes. God spoke to me and gave me the assurance I needed. How kind of Him to do this for me. Only God could have picked out the one verse in 31,102 verses that answered my need exactly when I asked for it. It just relieved me so much and now I could sleep. It has now been 10 years and I am cured, and He lived up to His words.

CHAPTER TEN
LITTLE BITTY PRAYERS

Most people don't realize that whatever is important to you is important to Him. Even if it's kind of silly if it is on your mind and you need help with it, he cares. It's like a little kid coming to one of their parents with some request that seems so trivial, but because your child asked for it, you help him/her if it's in their best interest. You don't laugh at them and tell them their need is silly and go away; of course not. God is like that too.

When I was in college at UAB, my assigned parking was about 5 blocks from campus. This day I was working at Baptist Montclair Hospital, but I had to go by one of my classes to get something that was really important, so I was going to stop by the school on the way home. At work, I got a Migraine headache. I had never had one before and never had one since. My head hurt so bad that it hurt to touch my hair. The pain was excruciating. I had to leave work, but I still had to stop at school. I don't remember what was so important, but it was something I had to get. On the way to UAB, it started raining so hard that I could not see. It was pouring down and I had to drive very slowly. Then I realized I had to walk 5 blocks from my parking lot with no umbrella to get to school. The rain got worse and my headache was killing me.

About 10 parking places were right next to the building I needed to go into. These were the most treasured parking places at UAB. I knew people who would get to work at 6:30 or 7 to get one of these spots even though they didn't start work until 8:00. Never in all my years at UAB (school and working) had I ever seen an open parking place here. I was at a red light about to turn onto the street where these parking places were. It was pouring rain and my head hurt so badly. I said, "God, I know this sounds stupid, but if you could make one of those parking places available, I would appreciate it so much." I knew this would be a literal miracle. Just as I turned onto the street, a car backed out of one of the spaces, and I pulled in. I only had a few feet to get into the building. God cared about something as tiny as a parking place because I was in need of that place. Nothing is too silly when God's children are in need.

I have had other times when I really **needed** some little thing, not wanted, but **needed** a little thing, and God has come through. Never think something is too small for God's attention.

CHAPTER ELEVEN
GOD AND MY BROTHERS

Both of my brothers died young. One from cancer at age 36 and one from an automobile accident at age 39.

When Johnny died from cancer, he had a 4-year-old little boy and his wife was pregnant. In his last weeks, he suffered in the hospital. My mother's heart was breaking every day watching this. I remember praying that God would take him and end his suffering and my mother's (and mine). But he lingered for 3 weeks. I was so mad at God. "Why are you doing this?" I kept asking. "What good is served by putting him and my mother through this? We all know the end results so what are you waiting for?" I was mad. Finally, on a Friday, I got a call to get to the hospital. I left work but got there right after he died. Rita was holding his hand when he died at 3 pm. As I left the hospital, I realized this was Good Friday, the day Jesus died, and he was supposed to die at 3 in the afternoon. Johnny died just when Jesus did. I realized this was why God's timing was right. What an honor by

God to die on the day his Son died and at the same time. We will always remember this, and God had a reason for his timing.

A few months later, we were at the beach for a week, and I really wanted to hear from God about Johnny. I believed Johnny was in heaven, but I just wanted to hear from him that he was ok since he left behind two small children, one he had never met. Each day, I took a walk down the beach, and because of my previous experience with the sand dollar, I asked God to let me find a whole white sand dollar as I walked the beach just to know Johnny was ok. I walked every day but found nothing. On the last day, I walked for a while and then headed back, thinking it was not going to happen. I remember saying to myself, "God, I guess you just don't want me to know." At that moment, right after that thought I looked down and right in front of my foot was a whole white sand dollar. Praise God! He did want me to know, after all.

Tommy was an alcoholic. I tried to get him in rehab and we were actually at the place when he backed out.

He was an alcoholic from about age 17 until his death. I talked to him so many times, but he couldn't quit and wouldn't do anything to help himself. Finally, I just said, "To hell with it." I'm done trying to stop someone from killing themselves. I didn't understand alcoholism that well and now I know it is a disease, but it is also curable if the person wants it to be. Tommy's behavior hurt my mother, which made me so mad at him.

Tommy never went to church, even though he was raised in the church. Tommy was not a mean person at all. He was always kind and willing to help others. Despite his drinking, he never missed work and he was one of their best employees.

When I was a pilot, I took him up flying one day. It was a fall day; the sun was very bright, and we were flying right into it. Air Traffic Control notified me there was a plane coming towards me at 12 o'clock (right in front of me), and its altitude was unknown. That meant we could be flying into a head-on collision and because the sun was so bright straight ahead, I could not see him, and no one knew his altitude. I stayed on heading, but reports from air traffic control said he was closing in on my position. I made a 90-degree turn to put myself (hopefully) at an angle that would assure our safety. It did.

When we landed, I told Tommy we could have been killed, and he could be facing God right then. What was he going to tell God that he had done for Him with his life? I witnessed him and tried to get him on a spiritual path with God. I had this wallet-size card called "Cross in my Pocket". It was laminated and had a little wooden cross on it with a saying about the cross and the sacrifice Christ had made for him. I gave it to him, and I was hoping he would keep it, but figured he would not.

Years later, on Good Friday, Tommy was killed in a car wreck. Remember, Johnny died on Good Friday also. He had a good car, but it was in the shop so he was driving an old junk car and as he took the exit off the interstate at Oxmoor road the front end of the car apparently started shaking so badly that he could not make the turn and he hit a power pole and was killed instantly.

One thing that consoled the family was he was on his lunch break and he had just left a rehab center where he had signed up to start treatment for his alcoholism. He made the decision on his own to change his life, and we were all proud of him for that. Maybe God knew that was good enough and took him. I really didn't know if Tommy was in heaven or not. He never acted on my request to start back to church; of course, he drank a lot. I had to go to the coroner's office and get his personal effects. I asked God to give me some kind of sign that Tommy was with him. When the coroner brought out his personal effects his wallet was included. Sticking out of the wallet about 2 inches (very obvious) was the card I gave him years ago, "Cross in my Pocket". I truly believe that was God's sign to me that Tommy was with him in heaven.

CHAPTER TWELVE
GOD AND HUMILITY

When my girls were about 7 and 9, we participated in delivering Christmas presents to underprivileged families. Me, Shari, and the girls were delivered to a home owned by a lady named Ms. Mabry. She was an older black woman who was raising a 2-year-old grandchild that had been abandoned by her mother and also raising her own daughter, who was about 8 years old. The house was a shack. I remember a small, shaggy Christmas tree sitting on a large propane heater which is all they had to heat the house. They had almost nothing. I will always remember looking at the light switch and seeing a dirty light plate around the switch that said "God Bless This House". I looked around at a shabby home and the thought that she would think to put that on the wall of such a place struck me deep in my heart. The gifts brought a lot of joy to the family. As we drove away, one of the girls said, Daddy, why do we only help these people at Christmas time?" I was convicted at that moment. I had no good answer to that question. I knew God was speaking to me. From that point on and for the next 30 plus years, we have helped this family financially. Whenever she calls and needs a prescription, we pay a bill or send her the money. One time, she called and wanted $75 to get her hair fixed so she would look good for some special church service. At first, I was hesitant in my mind about giving her money to go to the beauty shop. I mean, was that really a "need". But God spoke to my heart. I heard his words in my mind, "This lady has little money and can never afford to do something special for herself, something to make her look good at this special event." You have the money and you can do something to give her joy….do it". I gave her the money and was glad to do so.

Although it may seem we were helping her, in actual fact, she was helping us, especially me. Ms. Mabry talked all the time about how blessed she was (with almost nothing) and how good God was to her. She praised him constantly. No conversation occurred with her unless it was dominated by her love for the Lord. Her faith inspired me beyond words. She was a rock to me when my faith faltered. Although she had little money, she always bought me and Shari father's Day and Mother's Day cards. She was so excited about being able to do something for us. She would call a week ahead of time and tell us to be on the lookout for the cards. Then, she would follow up and make sure we got them. She was so proud to do something for us and we always made a big deal about it. Ms. Mabry has kept me humble. I truly believe she is an angel, sent to keep me humble and thankful for all that I have. Her faith is like one of the disciples and I know when she gets to heaven, the bible verse, "the last shall be first and the first shall be last will apply to her". She will sit on a throne in heaven. As noted, I don't believe in coincidences. God put her in my life and my family's life on that day we delivered the Christmas presents so she could guide me in faith and keep me humble.

CHAPTER THIRTEEN
GOD AND MY REGRETS

Like everyone I have done things I have regretted. But there is one incidence that regret the most and would give anything to have the chance to do it over.

My father was disabled and he was bed ridden very often for long periods of time. Sometime towards the later part of his life he was in the bed and he called me in and asked me to sit and talk to him. I honestly can't remember if I was still living at home or I was out in the working world but whenever it was I was very busy in my life. My response to him was short and curt, "what do you want to talk about? I asked in what was an obvious rushed tone. I certainly gave the impression that I was rushed and didn't really have the time. We may have talked a very short while but I wasn't trying to say anything to prolong the conversation. It ended up being short.

I know now he was suffering, lonely and wanted his son to be by his side and just talk but I was "too busy" I am so ashamed of myself for that moment in my life. I was so selfish, so self-centered that all that mattered was me and whatever it was that I thought was more important. I am just so, so ashamed of myself and I have cried over this incident (as I am doing now) and begged God and my daddy to forgive me for not recognizing that my daddy needed me and I was essentially not there.

Please let this be a lesson to each of you. NEVER let yourself be "too busy" to take a moment to be there for a loved one. It may not seem important to you but to them it could be the most important thing in the world. Maybe it's a phone call just to check on a loved one for no reason when you have a lot to do. You will never know what an unexpected effort to reach out could mean to someone. Whenever you think or use the words. "I am too busy"… just hesitate a minute. Am I really too busy to attend to the need of a loved one of a friend … **ALWAYS think when you say the words; "I am too busy."**

CHAPTER FOURTEEN
GOD, MY DADDY AND A GOOD TIME

I have already mentioned the good times my family had on vacations when my Dad was not sick. When he got sick he had a hard time participating in some of our sports activities. But I remember one time when I was so, so proud of him.

When I played Little League, or it might have been Pony League, each coach would get to draft players for their team. If you were the coach's son you automatically got to be on his team. My coach wanted me on his team, but he was afraid some other coach would get me before he could. He came up with this idea of my daddy, who was disabled, to be the assistant coach so I would automatically be on his team. I think everyone knew my

Dad's limitations and the whole thing was a plot just to get me on the team. Everyone felt my Dad was just a figurehead. He did help with the coaching, but it was very limited because of his health.

But one day he wanted to come to practice with me. I was catching batting practice and he said he wanted to pitch batting practice. Because he had heart problems besides other things, I was very concerned about him pitching, It was hot summertime, and the batting practice would last quite a while.

But he pitched and I was catching. He was GREAT! I was so proud of him. He pitched the whole batting practice, which was unusual since usually there was a relief pitcher. Almost every pitch was perfect and the idea that everyone thought he was a figurehead was gone as far as I was concerned. I know he had to push himself hard, but he never let on that he was tired......he was great and I was his proud son.

CHAPTER FIFTEEN
GETTING MY HANDS "DIRTY"

At Riverchase Presbyterian Church, they were always asking for people to help with projects, and if you couldn't help, then donate money. I always took the easy way out and gave money because I was too busy to take a day off work to help. One time, they needed some guys to move an older lady from the home she had lived in for years to a nursing home. Giving money wasn't an option so usually, in those cases, I just did not participate ... again because I was too busy.

This time I decided, for some unknown reason, to volunteer to help and take the day off of work. Taking a day off always paid you back with punishment because you would have tons of emails and voicemails the next day. Electronic access to emails was not available at that time, although I could listen to voicemails. We started at about 7 am by meeting at the church and then going to this lady's home. She was very emotional about leaving her home. Only now, at my age, can I appreciate how that hurt. We had to move big things downstairs and then upstairs when we got to the nursing home. It was grueling work, but somehow, there was an unexplainable joy in helping this lady. We did not finish until about 7 pm, and although exhausted, I had this tremendous feeling of joy. I can't explain how good I felt, but it was almost euphoric. I decided to stop at the grocery store on the way home to get some dinner. Again, everything just looked beautiful to me that night. When I returned to the car, I had a flat tire. Normally, after being so tired, I would have been cussing, but it did not phase me. I had no anger whatsoever. My feeling of pure joy stayed with me and changing the tire seemed to be a breeze. It was like I was floating on a cloud, and nothing could stop my happiness. I can't explain why my feelings were like that other than God or his angels were blessing me for helping ... **getting my hands dirty** helping another person instead of the easy way out of writing a check. I am so glad I did not say I was "too busy". I have no idea what I was dealing with at work that day, but I do remember this great feeling of helping others to this day.

Chapter Sixteen
God and Raising Children

Raising children has taught me more about God than any other experience. I see the relationship between a Father/Mother and their children exactly the way God (The father) looks at us (his children). Anytime I was searching for what to do in a situation with my children, I would look at it from the point of view of how God would handle that with me. Anytime my girls would want me to do something little like throw a ball or bounce them on my knee, I could rationally think this is not important, I need to be doing something else. In the scope of everything I had on my mind, was this something worthy of my time? I could rationalize that it wasn't important. But the point is it WAS important to them. Very important. It meant a lot to them and I would take the time to do whatever little thing it was. I learned that God is just like that. Things that are important to us, even if they are little, insignificant things, are important to God. Why? Because we are the most important thing in the universe to God, just like my children were the most important thing in my universe. You know how much you love your children, but that can't hold a candle to how much God loves you. Just learning to compare how I would handle a situation with my children by looking at how God would handle an equivalent issue with me was a great teaching point.

CHAPTER SEVENTEEN
CHRISTMAS

Christmas has always been a magical time for me. It goes back to my childhood. I remember my mother and Dad telling me that if you quit believing in Santa Claus, you wouldn't get any presents at Christmas. I wasn't taking any chances so I believed until I was like 11 or 12, and finally, my daddy told Rita, we are going to have to tell that kid the truth. He is too old to believe in Santa Claus and I am sure his friends don't, so we don't want them laughing at him. They broke the news, but once I realized there was no Easter Bunny that could bring all that candy, I knew there was no Santa Claus but never wanted to admit it just to make sure I got toys for Christmas. All that doesn't have much to do with God, but here is what does, and here is why I find Christmas so magical. As noted, my family had little money and struggled to make house payments and put food on the table.

Since I figured out the Santa Claus thing much earlier than I told anyone, I always worried we would not have enough money to have presents for Christmas. But through the grace of God, we always had a wonderful Christmas, with everyone getting great presents. How did my parents do this? They always came through for me and my brothers. I know God had a hand in it because gifts came that I never thought would be there. I just find magic in Christmas to this day. I am very childlike when it comes to Christmas. I love Christmas movies where unexpected wonders occur. It all comes back to God making a wonderful Christmas out of our nothing. He made Christmas extraordinary for ordinary people like us who had very little.

I am still a sentimental old fool about Christmas. Every Christmas, we decorate our house completely inside and out, even though no family and very few others ever see it. Shari does almost all the work (I bet you could have guessed that), and I appreciate her so much for tolerating my desire to have everything out for Christmas. We still decorate the tree with ornaments that I had as a small child. They must be 65+ years old and they are not pretty, but I love them. Many nights or early mornings, I sit and look at the Christmas tree, all our Santa Claus collections, and the other decorations and relive Christmas times from the past. These memories are priceless; I thank God that I can recall so much about so many Christmas days from my past.

CHAPTER EIGHTEEN
SOME GOOD INVESTMENTS

...

My wife has always loved horses since she was a child. As a little kid, she had a "stick pony" that was her special pet. The love affair with horses has remained with her during her entire life.

In 1986, we were newly married, and we were vacationing in Panama City Beach, Fl. While there, we saw some new condos located right on the beach that were just completed. We decided to go in and look at the "model condo". It was beautiful, and I never thought my wife would be interested, but she loved it, and we were going to buy it. It was a three-bedroom, three baths for $124,500. We felt it would be a good investment for the future. As noted earlier, I have always loved the ocean, and a place on the beach was a dream come true. But on our drive home, my wife said, "Why don't we look at getting into the horse business instead of buying the condo?" I asked if we could make money in that business, and she assured me we could. We would raise, breed, and show horses. OK, I gave in.

Well, financially, the long and short of it is we were in the horse business for 18 years and made $1500 ONE year. Now, that condo would have been worth at least $800,000 at its peak. So, I tell everyone I lost about $700,000 in the "horse business!

Financially, that is the bad news. But over the years, we owned many Arabian horses, and my wife loved to spend her Saturday's riding. The horse brought her great joy that you could never put a price on. We took the children out to where the horses were boarded to give them some feel for life on a horse ranch. One night turned out to be very special. One of our horses, Pinky, was having a foal (a baby). They called us about 9 PM and said if we wanted to watch the foal be born, we needed to get out to the barn. It was quite a drive, but we took the kids and went. I nor my children had ever seen anything like this. So, about midnight Pinky gave birth, and we got to video it. In my audio portion, I made the comment that this was a "really rare sight". It was, and I am so glad, we all witnessed one of God's miracles.

In the end, spending the condo money on a horse brought great pleasure to my wife and family. There is no price you can put on something like that.

In 1998, we once again looked at buying a condo on the beach. There was a beautiful high rise being built in Destin, Fl, right in the middle of the "action"

We looked at one of the finished models and decided to buy it. It was very expensive for us at that time, so we were going to have to put it on the rental program to pay for it. I did not feel good about our salesperson. He was like a used car salesman. I studied the numbers on projected rentals, and they just seemed too good to be true. Still, what did I know about condo rentals? Maybe he was right? I wanted it, but something kept nagging me, making me feel uncomfortable. We got right down to closing, and it was always like something was telling me not to do it. We backed out at the last minute, and the salesperson was pissed!

After the condo was completed, all the stucco came off this multi-story building, and each resident was assessed $100,000 to repair it. The builder had skipped town as had everyone associated with the project. The rumor was it was a mafia-backed project. The one guy I met seemed like he would fit into that organization. Looking back, I honestly believe the "Holy Spirit" was guiding me away from the purchase, knowing what the future held. The "Holy Spirt" was saying, "Don't do this."

In about 1999, we made another trip to the beach to look at buying a lot across the street from the beach. The lot was on a lake that was interconnected to the gulf. Only three other places in the world have these lakes, called Dune Lakes. This made the lot an attractive location. The price was low for a lot like this, so we were a little suspicious but thought we were getting a great deal. The land we would be building on had a good bit of "wetlands," which is a protected property, but the builder assured us he built on wetlands all the time and it would be no problem. I decided to get a land engineer to come look at the property and give me his opinion, so we made another trip to the beach to meet with him and the builder. Before the meeting, we pulled into a public beach parking lot to pray about the meeting. Basically, we said, "Lord, we have no idea what we are doing. Would you give us a CLEAR signal about what we should do? Buy the lot or not. Something we will know is a message from you". We met the builder who was gung-ho to promote the lot and build on it. The engineer was quiet and just listened. The land was like marshland. The engineer picks up a reed, which of course, is flimsy. He took the reed and pushed it into the very soft soil with one finger. He looked at me and said, "Son, if I were you, I would take money and go somewhere else." Bingo! That was our message. We didn't buy the land. Years later, someone built on that lot, but it was a major project to prepare the land. Also, you couldn't walk on the land around the house because it was a marsh. My grandkids would not have been able to get into the yard or fear of snakes or worse. It would have been a terrible lot. Thank you, Lord, for sending us that clear message.

CHAPTER NINETEEN
GOD AND GETTING OLDER

There is a saying that 'getting old is not for sissys.' This is true because as you age, things that used to work great now don't work that well. But it is important to recognize that God has promised to be with us throughout our lives and actually make us wiser when we are older than when we were young.

"I will be your God throughout your lifetime -- until your hair is white with age. I made you, and I will care for you. I will carry you along and save you"

(Isaiah 46:4).

"Therefore we do not lose heart. Though outwardly we are wasting away, yet inwardly we are being renewed day by day."

(2 Corinthians 4:16)

I wish Paul had not used the words "wasting away". Maybe he could have said we are "slowing down" or something a little nicer. But the second part means our spiritual knowledge is being renewed each day. That is what is important.

But I love God's words in Isaiah (above). He is with us all the way!

A lot of people struggle with aging. They try to fight it by getting plastic surgery to look younger or wear young girl's clothing styles. They want to be a part of the latest "fads" and be cool.

Really, you should strive to age gracefully. There is nothing wrong with trying to stay in shape and fit. As a matter of fact, it is a must that you make time to exercise. When you age, you MUST keep moving! I see so many people who do nothing physically and pay a dear price for it.

I have always been an exercise person simply because I think it is good for me. This started when I was about 26 years old. My resting heart rate was in the high 90's and I would get winded walking up a few steps. I decided to start running. I will always remember my first run was about 3 blocks! I worked my way up to running 4 miles per day about 4 times a week and I ran in a bunch of 10k races. I kept records of my progress to help motivate me. When I was working, we had a workout room in our office and I can remember ending my day about 6 or 630 PM and being really tired from work. I didn't feel like working out, but on my locker in the workout room, I had the Nike sticker "Just Do It." You don't know how many times seeing that made me stay and work out.

After I retired, I walked when I played golf (except in the hot summer), I worked out on my Nortek track or my Total Gym. I invented this exercise where I walk about thigh-deep in the ocean parallel to the beach for an hour. It's like water aerobics with weights on your legs. I like it so much I am thinking of getting a wet suit and doing it in the winter.

Now, despite all my efforts, there are things that I am limited from doing but I want to make those as few as possible. I really believe God wants us to do what we can to help ourselves enjoy aging. I have a saying on my desk that says, "Don't let what you can't do stop you from doing what you can do." I try to live by that.

One thing you learn when you are my age is that life is short no matter how long you live. If you dream of doing some trips, learning something new, or planning for an early retirement, then do it! You don't want to be on your deathbed, regretting not doing all the things you wanted to do.

Shari and I decided on a trip back from the beach in 1988 that we wanted to retire in 2003. We wrote out a financial plan, stuck to it, and accomplished the goal. I was 55, and she was 53 when we moved to the beach. Now, let's give credit where credit is due. God blessed us in many ways, or that would not have happened. He deserves the praise.

"In their hearts, humans plan their course, but the LORD establishes their steps." (Proverbs 16:9)

Retirement, especially when the kids were little, has been the happiest time of my life. I still have a game for a lifetime, golf, and so many other things that I have been blessed with.

I do know people who continue to work into their late 60's or early 70's. Some do it because they have to, some because they love their work. No one can fault people for doing this. But some who have tons of money keep working just to make more money. They could be doing so many other interesting things and helping others, but it's all about having a lot of money. An extremely wealthy man who no one liked recently died down here. Most people couldn't stand him because he was such a jerk. Many said they were glad he was dead. What an epitaph. I know another man who is extremely wealthy who is also disliked universally. He is an asshole from the word go. His son is an adult but has been in all kinds of trouble, but he buys his son's way out. He is a powerful businessman and tries to bully people into doing what he wants. He is a short guy, and once he stood up in a meeting and said," I may be short, but when I stand on my money, I am taller than all of you." He is so arrogant and universally disliked.

God tells us to never get too full of ourselves because we will be forgotten one day.

Why, you do not even know what will happen tomorrow. What is your life? You are a mist that appears for a little while and then vanishes.

(James 4:14-15)

Never make money your God.

Age gracefully.

More important than any of this physical conditioning or planning is spiritual conditioning.

Dealing with God is not different than any other thing in life. You get out of it what you put in it. I have found that teaching a Bible class at my church and attending bible studies has enriched my knowledge of God. Just going to church for an hour each week is making little investment and you will get little returns. It's sitting down with others who are seeking to understand God that will bring you treasures and a closeness to God that is unimaginable.

Bottom line on getting old; keep moving even when you don't feel like it. Study God's word with other Christians. I have learned that they know less or no more than me, so don't be intimidated by attending a bible worship.

Also, when you retire, you have to know what you are going to do all day. After a hectic life of never having enough time all of a sudden, you have time. I have seen too many people flunk retirement because they had nothing to do. It's very unhealthy.

I decided I wanted to give back because God had allowed me to retire so early. I had no idea what that would be. One day at my church, I was approached by a lady who was starting an organization to provide medical and dental care to children who did not have the ability to pay. She wanted me to call on doctors and dentists and ask them to see these children for free. I did not think this would work. I did some research and found others had failed to try this same endeavor. My doctor friends told me it would not work. I was doubting Thomas and told the organizers that I didn't see much chance for success. While contemplating what to do, I came home and while sitting at my desk, I saw a sign Robbie had given me as a retirement present. It said, "Make a Difference." I felt like this was God speaking to me. I did do the job, got 96 doctors and dentists to see the kids for free, and up to this date, we have provided free medical and dental care to over 11,000 children. Some of the stories are heartbreaking, but we have created many happy endings that literally changed the lives of these children. It is, without a doubt, the greatest thing I have ever done. I still work with the organization after 18 years.

When the time comes, enjoy yourself, but remember you have a lot to offer those who cannot help themselves. Don't miss the opportunity.

CHAPTER TWENTY
WHAT MAKES ME MOST HAPPY

The thing that brings the most joy in my life is the fact my family are all Christians. This goes back to the way my parents raised me in the church and I raised my girls in the church. That day with the Sand Dollar had a lot to do with this because of my promise to God to raise the girls in the church. There were many a Sunday morning where we had to drive from Rita's house to Riverchase Church, which took about 30- 35 minutes. Getting them up, getting breakfast, combing tangles out of little girls' hair, getting them dressed, and yes, I actually could braid their hair. There were a lot of big chores each Sunday morning and the girls did not always cooperate. There was usually some fussing and fighting on the way to church and I always felt like I had lost whatever religion I had by the time we got there, as the process was exhausting. Invariably, Staci would fall asleep about 10 minutes before we got there and when she woke up at church, she was grumpy as a snake. I had to sit between them in church (before they let the kids go to kids church about mid-service), and they were always wiggling and creating a distraction. I breathed a sigh of relief when the children's church started. People around us may have also.

We had a dedication of the church, and each member and family member got to sign a proclamation document. That Document would be hung on the wall for everyone who entered Riverchase to see. Now Staci's printing was not very good. I wondered if her name would be even legible. But Staci practiced writing her name for several weeks so she would do a good job. When it became her turn to sign, she was very meticulous and the way she wrote her name was just beautiful! I was so proud of her, and I think God was proud of her too. I have a copy of that document to this day.

I think they have great memories of Riverchase Church, as this is where God planted the seed for them to become Christians. They later did the same with their children.

I say all this because the fact we are all Christians means I will be with my family forever, thanks to Jesus. Nothing in the world makes me happier than knowing we will never be separated and we will live in heaven together … forever.

CHAPTER TWENTY ONE
CLOSING

Well, if you read this far, you know more about me than you used to. Most of all, I hope you see how God has been extraordinary in my ordinary life. I want you to see the same in your life. Consider This; Write your own story. Your family will cherish it.

Don't look at any day as an ordinary, uneventful day. God is always orchestrating things in your life, but you have to take the time to notice. Reflect on each day and see where God may have made some small move that benefited you.

Slow down just a little. Take time to enjoy what is all around you. You know, when I retired, I really had some time and I started looking at all the beautiful flowers Shari had planted in front of our house. Shari worked so hard to plant these flowers and make our yard look good, but honestly, I had never given them a second thought. Now, when I look at them closely, I am fascinated by how gorgeous each one is. God's creation of flowers was awesome and I almost missed it all. It's that kind of stuff that is all around you, but most of us, and I have sure been guilty of this, never give it a second thought. God's world is beautiful and if you give it a chance what was ordinary becomes extraordinary … especially your own daily life.

"Pops" Roberts

Made in United States
Orlando, FL
03 October 2023

37517204R00049